Turning Goblets

with Mike Cripps

Text written with and photography by Jeffrey B. Snyder

Schiffer Publishing Ltd

77 Lower Valley Road, Atglen, PA 19310

Dedication

To hobby wood turning enthusiasts everywhere.

Copyright © 1996 by Mike Cripps

Printed in Hong Kong

ISBN: 0-7643-0033-4

Library of Congress Cataloging-in-Publication Data

Cripps, Mike.
    Turning Goblets/Mike Cripps.
      p. cm.
     ISBN 0-7643-0033-4 (paper)
     1. Turning. 2. Goblets. I. Title.
TT203.C 1996
684'.08--dc20   96-15554
               CIP

Acknowledgments

I would like to extend my thanks to the following suppliers of hardwood and materials:
    Wagon House Hardwood Lumber, Route 52, Mendenhall, Pennsylvania. Phone: 1-610-388-6352; fax: 1-610-388-1772. Wood Craft, 210 Wood County Industrial Park, P.O. Box 1686, Parkesburg, West Virginia 26102-1686. Toll free phone number: 1-800-225-1153; fax: 1-304-428-8271.

Published by Schiffer Publishing, Ltd.
77 Lower Valley Road
Atglen, PA 19310
Please write for a free catalog.
This book may be purchased from the publisher.
Please include $2.95 postage.
Try your bookstore first.

We are interested in hearing from authors
with book ideas on related subjects.

Contents

Foreword

I have known Mike Cripps for many years and it is a particular pleasure to introduce him to you as the author of this book. He is a big hearted, jovial and highly talented turner who is particularly suited to lead you through the techniques he describes.

Mike and I first met at one of his early wood turning meetings held at a local Cricket Club. His enthusiasm for turning and willingness to help others encouraged a lot of members to improve technique and try other projects.

About a year later, after a lot of hard work, Mike became one of the founder members of the A.W.G.B. (The Association of Woodturners of Great Britain) which was launched in 1987 at the first Loughborough seminar.

In 1990, after being made redundant, Mike decided to set up his own turning school/wood and tool store. This has been a great success and hundreds of aspiring turners have passed through his classes, some now winning competitions, a tribute to Mike's teaching skills and encouragement.

The project in this book is good practice for any turner - just follow Mike's superb instructions and enjoy your turning.

Mac Kemp
Chairman
Middlesex Wood turners Association

About this Book — Turning Goblets

Goblets are fun to make, and turning them is interesting because it involves both spindle turning and bowl turning. I use the first project in this book (which is a simple goblet with a trumpet foot) to demonstrate the use of several tools and alternative methods so you may choose the way that suits you and the equipment that you have.

The second project in this book is to make a tall goblet with a straw stem. Do not try to tackle this project first thing in the morning after over-indulgence the night before, or when you are shaking with temper after an argument! Get yourself totally relaxed — imagine that you are a great artist and tackle this rewarding task with great delicacy and finesse. When you have completed your first straw-stemmed goblet, make another one even longer and thinner, then repeat the process again and again. Who knows where this artistic dedication could lead you? (Probably up to your armpits in tall, wobbly goblets!)

By now you will welcome the ultimate challenge of tackling the third project in this book — making a chalice from specially selected wood. This project is made in three pieces; this is a more effective way of utilizing very high quality timber. A chalice is described in the English dictionary as "a drinking cup used in celebrations." So why not celebrate once you have made all the pieces in this book.

How many times have you been standing in front of the lathe in the workshop thinking, "What shall I make?" and surprise, surprise, nothing has sprung to mind. In this book you have the benefit of seeing three vessels beautifully illustrated in high quality colour pictures. There are numerous sketches of alternative shapes together with a photographic gallery of pieces I and some of my wood turning colleagues in England have made.

Common Sense Information for Beginners to Wood turning

Obtaining Knowledge

Before turning wood on your own, make the effort to watch someone else doing it and do not be afraid to ask questions. Most people that I have met who work in wood are friendly and are usually only too pleased to help someone starting in this rewarding hobby. Books and videos are, of course, a great way of obtaining knowledge of the subject; however, the best ways to learn are either to take a 'Beginner's Course' or get some hands on experience if you can.

Buying Your First Woodlathe

I am often asked, "Which lathe should I buy?" My answer is always "Get the best that you can afford." Cheap imported lathes very often are noisy, this being caused by inferior electric motors that vibrate excessively. This vibration reverberates through the drive belt to the lathe headstock, which is usually clad in a thin, rattly casing. This vibration can be reduced by easing the tension on the belt slightly and making sure all bolts and screws, including the bench securing bolts are tight. It is well worth the effort to check them over before using the machine.

Whether you buy new or second-hand, when looking for a reliable machine the following points are worth your consideration:

(a) has it got a heavy steel plate or cast head?
(b) are the head and tailstock spindles hollow to allow the use of standard fittings (1 or 2 morse tapers)? This will save money as you will be able to buy 'off the shelf' lathe accessories.
(c) place a drive centre in the headstock and a centre in the tailstock and check for alignment with the points. If they do not meet properly you will always drill oversized holes and have excess vibration.
(d) place a mandrel or large accessory such as a drill chuck in the headstock and check for sideways movement. If the lathe has standard bearings, movement denotes a worn bearing. If, however, bearings are tapered roller types this could be cured by adjustment.
(e) check for side play in the tailstock where it located on the bed. If badly worn, this will cause you to drill inaccurately and will cause vibration.
(f) make sure that the tool rest locks on the bed and in its support securely and without excess force on the securing levers. REMEMBER that you frequently move the tool rest.
(g) if buying second-hand, take a mental calculation of the chucks and accessories that come with it, usually it is the presence of these that makes a used lathe an attractive proposition as a new wood turning chuck can cost around $150 to $200. A drill chuck and live centres cost around $50 and drives and man-

drels $20 to $30 each when purchased new.
(h) smell the motor to check for any burnt smells which denote it is already burnt out or on the way. Also, disconnect the belt and see if it runs quietly. A noisy motor usually means the bearings on the shaft need replacing.

Basic Turning Tools

The ROUGHING GOUGE, as the name implies, is used for roughing down square to round. It is also used for the preliminary shaping work on spindle turning e.g. shallow curves and tapers. I find that it is an excellent tool for flat areas when face plate turning as well.

A 3/4" roughing gouge is the ideal tool to start with. The approach to the wood should be as follows. Place the roughing gouge firmly on the tool rest with the blade pointing upwards. Lower the tip of the tool down slowly until the bevel rubs on the wood without the cutting edge coming into contact with the wood (this is what I call the no-cut position). Continue to lower the cutting edge down onto the wood until you obtain the first sign of a shaving. Only when this is obtained should you travel along the tool rest from left to right and vice versa to true up the wood between centres.

The PARTING TOOL is an essential tool. I would suggest that a 1/8" wide parting tool is the best to start with and will be the cheapest for spindle turning. The parting tool is used to make incisions into the wood at each end of a piece to provide a waste end which is discarded when the piece is parted off the lathe.

This tool can be used in two ways but when making deep parting cuts or grooves, always ensure that you make the cuts slightly wider than the tool so that it does not get gripped. One method is pointing the tool upwards while sitting it firmly on the tool rest and pushing it in an upward direction. A second method is to start with the tool again sitting on the rest and slowly levering the tip downwards using the tool rest as a fulcrum. NEVER go below the level position and point the tool downwards as it could be pulled in towards the wood and jammed against the tool rest.

The parting tool is also useful for rolling beads and cutting recesses for chucks on faceplate work. If the parting tool is used on its side, flat on the tool rest, the point can be used for scoring decorative grooves in the wood using this scraping cut.

SPINDLE GOUGES come in a range of sizes from 1/8" to 3/4". Most commonly today they are made from round section bar but traditional or continental gouges are still being produced. These are made from pre-formed curved section steel.

The main uses for the spindle gouges are for forming beads and coves, rounding over and squaring up end grain. I would suggest a 3/8" is a good one to start with.

When cutting coves or hollows, point the centre of the gouge at the starting point, cutting down one side to just past the centre of the bottom of the cove and then repeat the process on the other side. By cutting down the hill, or from the largest toward the smallest diameter, you will be compressing together the fibres in the wood with the bevel while the cutting edge does its job. This will give you a good finish. Cutting uphill separates the fibres and leaves an inferior finish. REMEMBER, if you slowly swing the end of the handle in a circular motion, the shape of the cove will also have a round profile. To cut beads or balls, the tool has to be rolled over working again from the top toward the bottom with the bevel rubbing.

The SKEW CHISEL is probably the tool that takes a fair bit of practice before it is mastered. I would suggest that you purchase a 1" OVAL SKEW as this is a size that is good for planing and making beads and squaring ends. An oval skew is nicer to handle than a rectangular section skew as the corners tend to stick on any nicks or grooves in the tool rest.

To plane a cylinder to a smooth finish, raise the tool rest to centre height and position it as close as possible to the pre-roughed out cylinder. Place your thumb firmly on the tool rest just past the end of the wood and tuck the skew between the thumb and the tool rest. Now, using the short corner of the skew and not using any more than 1/8" from the point, the tool should be about 45 degrees to the wood. Obtain a shaving and travel along the tool rest. You may have to alter the angle of the tool or raise or lower the blade slightly. REMEMBER the shaving is the reward and the sign that you are cutting correctly. You will be able to cut coming back along the tool rest by holding the tool at the same angle.

To form beads with the skew I prefer to use the long point and as when cutting only use the actual point and up to 1/8" from it. NEVER cut uphill. Start at the top of the bead, rolling the skew over as it cuts through 90 degrees with the blade vertical on completion of the cut at the base of the bead. When making beads or spheres, work on the right then the left, repeating the process and bringing on both sides together. REMEMBER when cutting over beads etc., rub the bevel all the way — lifting the handle up as the cutting action goes down.

The BOWL GOUGE, as the name implies, is the tool for turning bowls. A 3/8" high speed steel gouge made from 1/2" round steel with a long and strong handle is the best size to buy. I maintain a bevel of approximately 45 degrees and remove the sharp corners the makers provide by grinding two long blades on the top of the gouge.

Although I love to use the bowl gouge for spindle turning, particularly for long flowing curves for goblets and vases, its main use is for bowls and facework. It is important to constantly rub the bevel to support and steady the cutting edge around external and internal curves. Cutting with the tip unsupported by the bevel makes it 'grabby' and prone to digging in.

To find the right position, lay the bevel on the wood (making sure the tool is firmly on the tool rest) so that you are in the 'no cut' position. With the bevel in contact with the rotating wood, slowly raise the handle until a shaving appears. Stay with it and guide it along or round the surface of the object you are making. You will soon appreciate the supported feeling that the bevel provides as the gouge tip cuts. REMEMBER, if you are changing the shape of the wood from a square corner to a curve, it is much easier if you cut away the corner to a wide chamfer first. To cut wood without the bevel rubbing is like driving a car without wheels!

All the tools that I have just written about are cutting tools which are usually used in an upward mode with the SKEW chisel being the exception as by raising the tool rest it is usually used mainly with the toolrest in the 'level with centre' position.

I would strongly recommend that you buy good quality tools. For the tools we have discussed so far — ROUGHING GOUGE, PARTING TOOL, SKEW CHISEL, SPINDLE GOUGE and

BOWL GOUGE — I feel that it is worth the extra cost to purchase high speed steel. Tools of high speed steel will hold their edge up to five times longer and will not be affected like carbon steel by overheating from the electric grindstone.

The last of the basic tools to talk about are SCRAPERS, which are mainly used to remove any bumps and ridges left after using the Bowl Gouge. A scraper is used in a downward position with the tool rest set back from the work to give room to use it at this angle. When sharpened correctly a sharp burr of metal stands up proud on the end of the tool which will produce plenty of shavings.

I have found that carbon steel scrapers, which are less expensive than high speed steel, work extremely well. The burr can be raised by pressing a hard metal bar across the end of the scraper which forces the cutting edge burr upwards (this is known as using a ticketer).

Scrapers can be made in different shapes. For faceplate work a square ended scraper, say 1" to 1 1/4" across with the corners relieved to allow the movement of the tool from the centre to the edge of flat surfaces and vice versa, is ideal. By grinding the corners back slightly, snagging is avoided when in use. For inside bowls and open vessels a 1" to 1 1/4" ROUND NOSED SCRAPER is ideal. The metal should be as sturdy as possible to avoid vibration when cantilevering inside a bowl on the tool rest.

Sharpening the Tools

The SKEW CHISEL and the PARTING TOOL only need re-grinding occasionally and honing with a slipstone is all that is required but keep them sharp at all times. A slipstone made from metal impregnated with diamond dust is an effective way of sharpening them.

I sharpen the end of the ROUGHING GOUGE to a shallow bevel of approximately 45 degree - REMEMBER, although useful for turning softwood etc. long bevels are more grabby for beginners to use. Be very careful to keep the blade straight across by rolling the tool over on the grinding wheel from one corner to the other. A common fault with new turners is only to sharpen the rounded part of the cutting edge which, if done for several sharpenings, forms two long points like cats ears on the gouge.

I sharpen the SPINDLE GOUGE to a finger nail shape with a bevel angle of somewhere between 45 degrees to 60 degrees. If you hold the gouge upwards and rotate it on the grindstone from left to right you will very quickly form a sharp point on the Spindle Gouge and lose the rounded profile. To avoid this rotate the tool, sharpening from centre to right following the existing finger nail shape. You will find that in doing this when you start (with the handle straight and in line with the grindwheel) when you finish the handle will be approximately 45 degrees to the right of you. Now repeat this process from the centre to the left. ALWAYS use only light pressure — only a small touch on the stone is required. It is a good idea to practice this manoeuvre with the grinder switched off first.

The BOWL GOUGE is sharpened in much the same way but if you want the cut back profile I use on my bowl gouges, start from the middle and, following the edge of the tip profile, roll the gouge right over so the flute is facing the wheel, pushing it upwards. Then, to sharpen the cutback section, sharpen as before going toward the other side.

I always use SCRAPERS with the manufacturer's name uppermost so I know which way to use it; however, when sharpening these tools on the grindstone, I turn them upside down. Because the stone is rotating toward you and downwards, it naturally forms a good burr on the bottom edge of the tool which, of course, becomes the top when you use it.

Your grindstone should be kept at a sensible height so that you can use it without stooping. Mine is about 4' from the ground. It is a great help to have an anglepoise light on the stone. The following safety tips should be observed:

(1) NEVER use a grinder without eye protection e.g. visor, goggles or safety glasses. I find that those little clear plastic windows that are provided very soon get scratched and become impossible to see through.

(2) NEVER work on a grindstone that is clogged or out of true. Diamond Wheel Trimmers are much less expensive now and they clean the stone and trim it in just a couple of passes. REMEMBER a clean stone cuts cooler and sharpens efficiently. Take precautions by wearing a mask when trimming the stone as a large amount of dangerous dust is created when this is done.

(3) NEVER ever use your grindstone on soft or non ferrous metals such as copper or brass. If the stone is clogged with this type of material it can overheat with use and even shatter.

An alternative method for sharpening tools now being sold by a major British tool maker consists of wooden discs mounted on an arbor with aluminium oxide abrasives adhered to them. These can be held in a chuck on the lathe and you can clearly see what you are doing. The recommended speed is around 1400 r.p.m on a 5" disc.

Using the Lathe

Spindle Turning (or Turning Between Centres)

As a general rule I prefer to turn small diameter work (say up to 2" x 2") at a fairly fast speed. If you are reducing square stock to round, this makes the task quicker and avoids excess vibration being transferred through the tool to the joints in your hand.

Let us assume you have a piece of square timber mounted securely between centres. Select a speed of around 1200 to 1500 r.p.m. If we look at the pulleys contained within the headstock when selecting our turning speed, it is important to note that the smaller the size of the pulley, the faster the speed of the lathe will be. Put on your visor or safety goggles — ALWAYS PROTECT YOUR EYES.

Always avoid inhaling wood dust when sanding. Use a mask and an extraction unit. An airstream helmet is good but will not prevent a build up of fine dust in your workshop.

To mount the wood between centres when I am teaching, I use a ring centre or friction drive as opposed to a 2 or 4-prong drive. This method is safer because if you have a 'dig in' the wood will stop rotating and slip on the centres. A pronged drive keeps on going regardless and a heavy 'dig in' will result in chunks of wood flying off or the whole piece leaving the lathe. If you do not possess a friction drive, reduce the tension on the drive belt. This will also provide a safety mechanism.

Adjust your tool rest to around 1/2" below centre. Rotate the wood by hand before switching on to make sure it clears the tool rest. Then check all securing levers or nuts including the headstock swivel (applicable on rotating head lathes only) — the tool rest support to the lathe bed — the tailstock to the lathe bed and finally the securing lever to the quill of the tailstock.

Using a 3/4" or 1" Roughing Gouge, point the cutting edge upwards away from the rotating wood onto the tool rest. NOTE — NEVER place any turning tool onto the wood unless the tool is firmly on the tool rest first. Now, gently lower the tip of the gouge until the bevel (flat area next to the cutting edge) is rubbing on the rotating wood without cutting. As lightly as possible (I call this the no-cut position), and still with the gouge on the rest, lift the back hand up and look for the finest of shavings. Use only light pressure toward the wood and obtain a light buzz from the cutting edge as you ease the tool along the tool rest and back.

Stand in nice and close to the lathe with your feet apart and use body movement to move the tool from left to right and vice versa. REMEMBER, outstretched arms are wobbly things. Keep the inside part of your arm against your side and move the tool along with body movement only. As soon as a gap of, say, no more than 1/2" appears between the tool rest and the wood, stop the lathe and move the tool rest in as close as you can while checking that the wood rotates freely without rubbing on the tool rest.

Switch on and, while looking at the horizon (top edge of the wood), make a nice smooth cylinder. Do not allow the tool to swing — this will give you a bad shape. Obtain a shaving, keep the tool at this angle, and move along the tool rest.

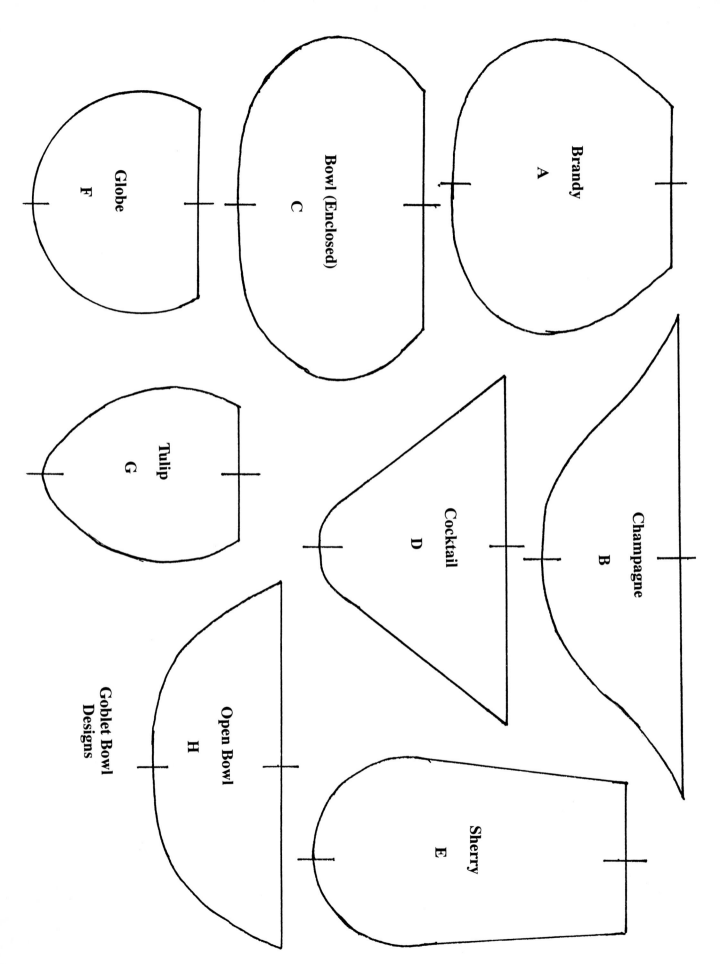

Brandy
A

Bowl (Enclosed)
C

Globe
F

Tulip
G

Cocktail
D

Champagne
B

Goblet Bowl
Designs

Open Bowl
H

Sherry
E

Goblet Patterns: Enlarge or reduce these patterns to fit the goblet size you wish to create. Mix and match bases with tops.

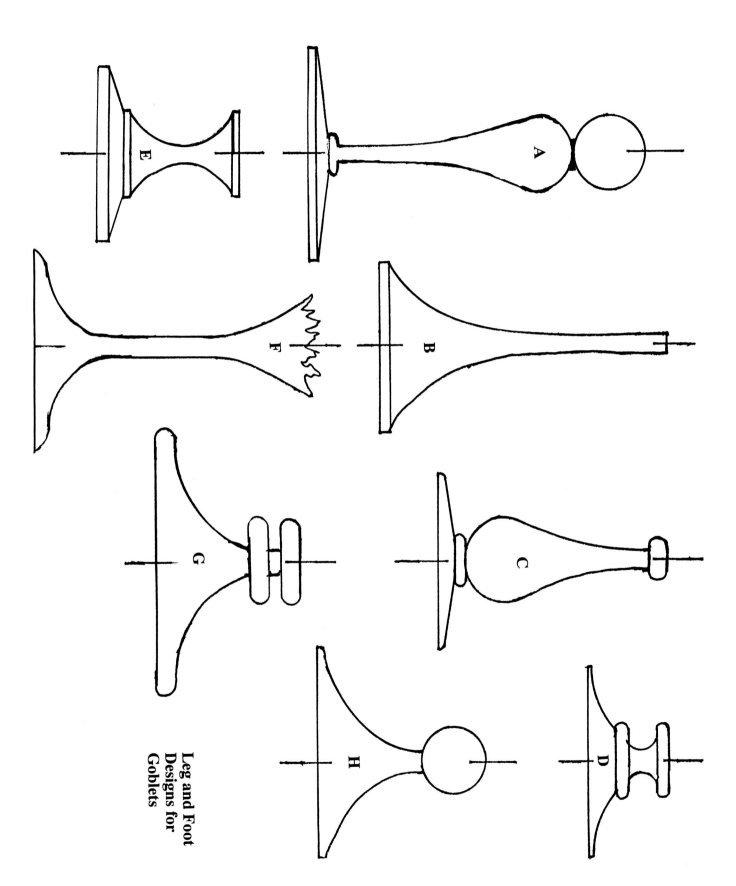

Leg and Foot Designs for Goblets

A ring centre, seen in place here on the lathe, is the best centre for beginners. It is most forgiving if you have a dig in.

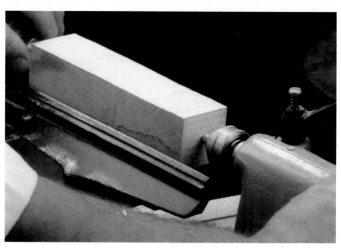

Mark the centre of the blank with a small hole made with an awl. On softer woods, tighten up the tail stock until the drive centre grips. For a harder piece of wood, we might have to tap the centre with a hammer to begin to drive it into the wood.

The smaller the pulley on the headstock, the faster the work is going to go.

Before you turn on the lathe, rotate the wood by hand to make sure that it is not hitting the tool rest. The top of the tool rest should be positioned approximately 3/4" below the centre. This height will vary according to the diameter of the timber, the height of the lathe, and the comfortable working postion the turner wishes to adopt.

Double check all of the locking handles to the tail stock, and the tool rest, making sure they are tight. This precaution will help you avoid accidents. If your lathe is of the swivel head type, make sure the swivel nut is tightened as well. Otherwise, the head could turn while the wood is spinning.

The Roughing Gouge:

Let's look at the tools now. The first of the tools is the roughing gouge. For people first learning to turn, the roughing gouge is much easier to use if the bevel edge is kept short, approximately at 45 degrees. Longer bevels may be preferred as a turner become more experienced. But in the hands of someone new to wood turning, a long bevel is both grabby and more difficult to use.

Begin with the tool in the "no cut" position.

The tool should be kept straight across at its cutting edge. I will explain this in detail later when we cover tool sharpening.

Raise your arm, lifting the handle until the blade just touches the wood and begins to form shavings.

Slowly move along the length of the wood. Only light pressure is required with a sharp tool. As you move along the wood, roughing the corners off, all you should hear is a light buzz. That is the sign that you are doing the job correctly, making a nice spray of shavings as you go. Keep the tool firmly on the tool rest. Ensure that the bevel of the tool is always rubbing against the wood, this stablizes the tool for you and makes it safer to handle as well as your tools will not need to be sharpened as often. Someone new to wood turning tends to stand a long way out from the lathe and work with arms extended, this tends to make the tool vibrate and wobble, making it hard to get a nice finish. Move in close. Keep your lower arm (the one holding the lower part of the handle) resting against your body, using your body to move the tool back and forth.

Remember, the slower you go, the nicer the finish, half of the rifling has been removed in this picture.

If you travel too fast, rifling will occur. Spiral grooves are created all along the wood.

The roughing gouge is mainly used to reduce square stock to round and for truing up unbalanced timber. However, the roughing gouge is also a useful tool for shaping shallow curves and hollows. Always work down the hill (from the largest to the smallest diameter). By doing this, you are compressing the fibers of the wood together and cutting the wood as it likes to be cut; cutting uphill will separate the wood fibers and give you an inferior finish.

A good parting tool to start turning with is a 1/8" parting tool. Later on, you may feel like investing in a diamond profile 3/16" parting tool (seen on the left) which moves more easily through the wood, without a tendency to be gripped. The diamond profile is, of course, also a much stronger tool for deeper cuts.

The approach to the wood, as before, is from a high position with the bevel rubbing. Lift the handle upwards and lower the cutting edge gently down onto the surface of the wood. Continue cutting into it, then go back to the starting position again and take a second cut alongside the first to widen the groove. This will prevent your tool being grabbed in a narrow parting cut. The first use of this tool is to remove

the scrap wood from either end of the piece. There are two reasons for doing this. One is to remove the marks left by the drive and live centres and the other is to ensure that the wood is cut away on the end of the piece of timber. This area is often full of small hair cracks where it has dried.

While parting the wood, never allow the tool to fall below the centreline position because it can be pulled in by the rotating wood and get caught between the wood and the tool rest.

The second method of using the parting tool is with it sitting firmly on the tool rest, the bevel rubbing, pushing upwards only. Again widen the groove as before to keep the tool from getting gripped.

Cut down the diameter of the waste wood so that it is a little larger than the lathe centres. This will keep the waste wood out of our way, giving us better access to the ends of the wood.

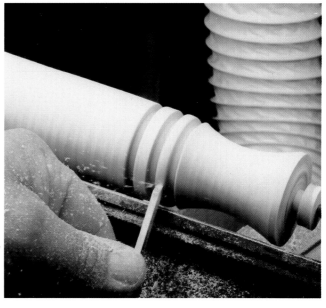

The parting tool is also very useful for forming beads. The wider the parting tool, the easier it is to use for this function. Make two shallow grooves, one on either side of the proposed bead. Place the parting tool with the bevel rubbing in the centre of the bead-to-be and, with a rolling action, roll over to the right two or three times until you have rounded over the square corner on the right.

Then move to the left to round the other side. Remember, always look at the horizon to obtain the best view of the shapes you are making.

The parting tool has one other useful function. Placed on its side, flat on the tool rest in a downward scraping mode, it is excellent for making fine decorative lines and grooves.

The Spindle Gouge:

The spindle gouge is used for generally shaping wood, forming coves and beads, and can be used to clean up end grain. The best spindle gouge for beginners is the 3/8". To make a cove, start with the bevel rubbing, supporting the cutting edge, and swing the handle in a perfect circular motion. If the handle travels in a circle, your cove will be round. Smooth flowing actions are the secret of nice shapes.

With the parting tool, we can further enhance the appearance of the cove by cutting two small shoulders, one on either side. This gives the cove a classical look often found in beautiful and period furniture.

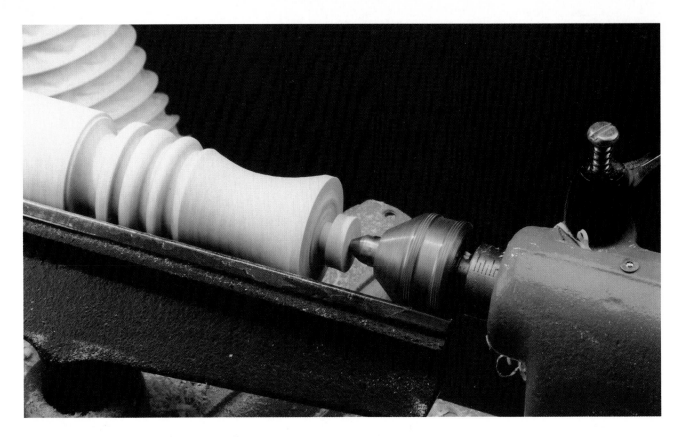

Raise the tool rest to the lathe centre height or just above centre to use the skew chisel.

I would suggest you buy a 1" oval skew chisel. You will find this tool much nicer to handle and much smoother to run along the tool rest than the old style square edged skew chisel. The square corners tend to catch in all the marks in the tool rest. The oval chisel glides across them.

Use the short corner of the skew for planing the wood. We are only going to use the area 1/8" from the short corner. Do not cut with the higher part of the blade.

First put your thumb slightly to the right of the starting position on the tool rest. Lay the bevel of the tool on, raise a shaving just above the short corner.

Slide the tool along the tool rest in a planing action. If the tool judders and doesn't run smoothly, either raise or lower your back hand slightly or change the angle of your cut very slightly. When you feel it is right, continue with the planing action.

Using the skew chisel to make beads.

The skew chisel is used for rounding over ends, forming balls and beads. To round the end you must rub the bevel along the edge of the wood.

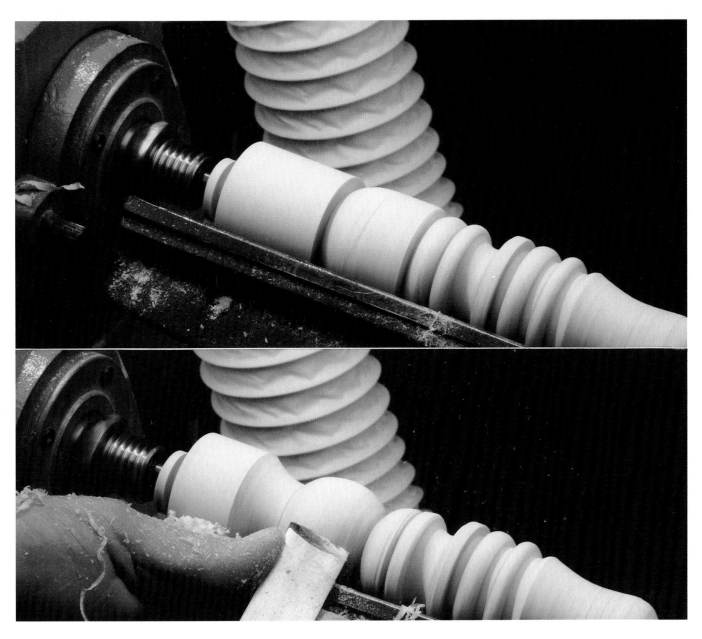

I am using the skew chisel to make a ball. Work first to the right and
then to the left, bringing the ball into shape on both sides equally.

The Round Nosed Scraper:

Buy a 1" or 1 1/4" round nosed scraper manufactured from good, sturdy metal. The scraper doesn't have to be made of high speed steel. The round nosed scraper, used in the downward angle, is ideal for cleaning up, removing tool marks, smoothing down troublesome end grain, and is invaluable when face plate or bowl turning.

The Bowl Gouge:

A 3/8" bowl gouge is a good size to start with in your tool kit. You can see how large this is.

Sharpening the tools using an electric grinding wheel:

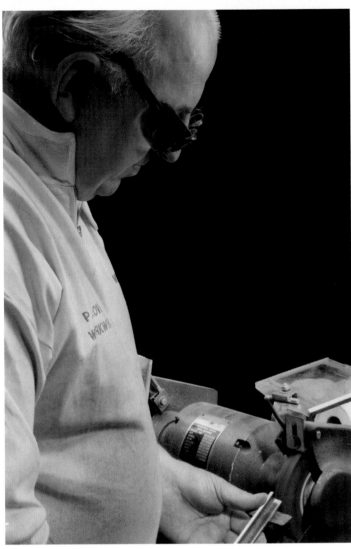

It is essential that your grindstone is fixed at a sensible height where you can view what you are doing without stooping. Standard work bench height is far too low for most people. The grindstone should also be well lit. Light is an essential aid when examining a tool for sharpness; a blunt section of the blade will reflect light and a sharp section will not. I prefer not to use the manufacturer's see-through shields. I find they soon become scuffed and marked and are very difficult to see through. Always wear safety goggles or glasses while working on the grindstone. This is very important. Always ensure that your grinding wheel is running true and that it is clean. Both of these functions can be achieved with the use of a diamond (or other form of) trimmer.

Sharpening the roughing gouge. Make sure the top is straight across.

Sharpening the spindle gouge. Refer to the notes in the general material for further sharpening details.

Turning Goblets

Trumpet Foot Goblet

To begin, we are using a block of American ash measuring 8" long and 4" square. Mark the centre prior to mounting it on the lathe. Mix and match bowls with bases to design the goblet of your choice.

Using a roughing gouge, begin by reducing the block to a smooth cylinder.

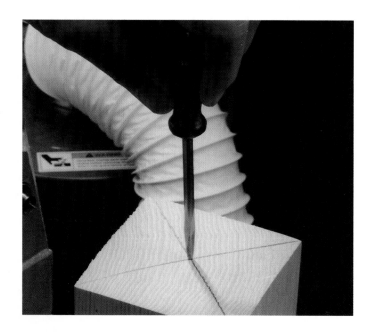

Use a awl to make a small hole in each end of the block. These holes will help fit the block onto the centres on the lathe.

Mark off the waste wood ends with a pencil.

Using a parting tool, reduce the waste wood. Bevel the edge of the wood slightly to make it safer to handle.

A scroll chuck is a good investment for the beginner because it has smooth contours on the edge and is very versitile as the jaws travel an inch in adjustment. It is very useful for gripping with compression on a spigot and with expansion in a recess. Using this chuck will be explained later in more detail. This project only requires holding in the compression mode.

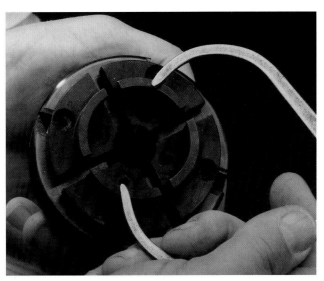

The next operation is to set a pair of calipers to size a spigot for holding the piece in the chuck on the lathe. Open the jaws slightly from the fully closed position to have some movement. When we buy calipers from the store, these are tools usually made for engineers and as such they have sharp points. It is much safer and easier to use calipers with these sharp ends rounded over so that they are not inclinded to grab on the wood.

The jaws are fully open.

Parting in the spigot. Make the opening wider than the parting tool so the tool doesn't get gripped.

Reduce the diameter of the waste wood with the roughing gouge.

Hold the calipers gently against the wood without pushing. When you reach the appropriate diameter of the spigot with the parting tool, the calipers should gently slide over the spigot's surface. If you are not happy with this, there is nothing wrong with stopping the lathe each time and measuring with the wood while it is stationary.

Reduce the remaining waste wood down to the size predetermined by the size of the calipers.

Prepare the spigot to the depth of the chuck jaws so that the wood will fit tightly into the jaws. Measure first the depth of the chuck, then — using the parting tool — reduce the end of the wood to fit.

When mounting the wood in the chuck, it is imperative that the jaws are tightened down securely using the tommy bar and the C spanner. Mount the wood into the chuck with firm pressure on the tommy bar and C spanner. Bring the tail stock up again. We will be doing as much tail stock supported work as possible.

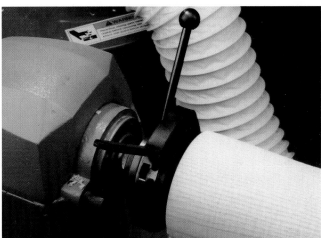

The wood is fit to the chuck.

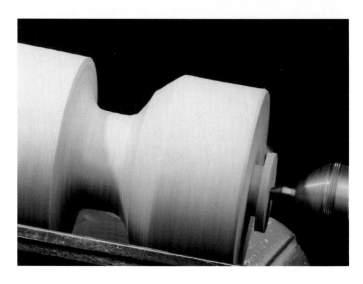

Using a 3/8" bowl gouge, make a circular cutting motion — with the bevel rubbing — and reduce some of the wood below the bottom of the goblet bowl.

Cut a 45 degree angle across the corner at the base of the goblet bowl before putting the external radius on. It is much easier than trying to convert a square corner to a radius.

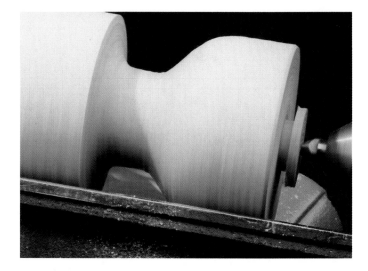

The rounded radius.

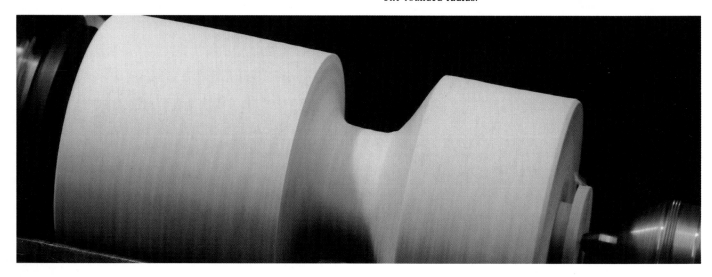

The reduced leg diameter. This provides better access to allow us to move the tool around the bowl.

Cut off the waste wood with the parting tool.

Remove the live centre; always remove the pointed centre from the tail stock when you move the tail stock away from the wood or you may hit your elbow and hurt yourself.

Begin working in from the edge now. Think about the rim of the goblet as you go.

Once you have moved the tool rest across the end to the goblet begin to open the centre with the bowl gouge.

The most common error of the beginning wood turner is the formation of a centre pimple. This is an area of wood we have missed with our gouge by cutting too high or too low.

Reducing the interior with the bowl gouge. Never cut past the centre point.

This pimple is created when the bowl gouge is not cutting into the very centre line of the goblet.

Raise the gouge slightly, aiming for the centre, and the pimple is removed.

The finished position in the centre. The gouge has pivoted around on the tool rest to the centre.

We are now forming the shape of the inside lip of the goblet.

Switch off the lathe and measure the depth of the goblet bowl.

This is the starting position of the gouge during the hollowing out process. The reason for this wide movement is to keep the bevel rubbing firmly on the wood while the cutting edge does its job. When cutting the end grain, if we don't rub the bevel and compress the fibers of the wood together as we cut, the fibers will be hooked out and a very rough finish will be obtained. To find the ideal position with the

gouge in a partly hollowed out piece, place the bevel on the wood in the inverted "no cut" position. Move the handle forward until the first sign of a shaving is formed and then proceed, with the bevel rubbing. To cut wood without the bevel supporting the cutting edge is like driving a car without wheels.

Transfer this measurement to the outside of the goblet, allowing roughly 1/4" to spare.

Switch the lathe on again and place a pencil mark around the goblet at this marked point. Part in now to determine the position of the external underside of the goblet.

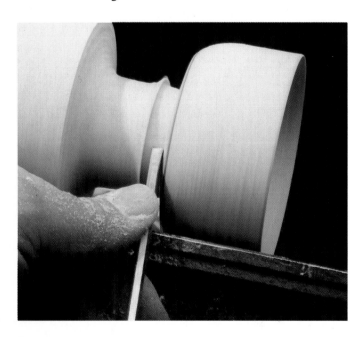

Sanding down the inside of the goblet. Use cloth-backed flexible abrasive from the coarsest to the finest grade and fill the centre of the abrasive strip with sawdust to avoid burning your fingers. Mark the back of the paper from one to six (coarsest to finest) to avoid confusion. Begin sanding with the coarsest abrasive you feel you need, starting from the centre and moving to the edge, wiping out the dust with each pass. It is very important that you don't hold the abrasive still at any time or you will score the piece, particularly with the coarser grades of abrasives.

To finish the inside of the goblet at this stage is most important, particularly if the goblet is to have a thin stem. Any pressure would cause a thin stem to break if it were completed before applying the finish.

Rounding the outside of the goblet to match the inside, using the bowl gouge.

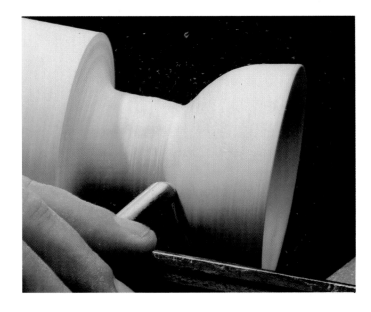

Check the thickness as you go with your fingertips.

Use the parting tool to reduce the lip just below the bowl.
Cut a curve in from the left with the bowl gouge to create space to allow the bowl gouge to get in to complete the shape of the bowl of the goblet.

The rounded bowl.

Rounding the bowl of the goblet with the bowl gouge.

Apply oil to the outside of the goblet bowl and buff dry with a paper towel or a soft cloth.

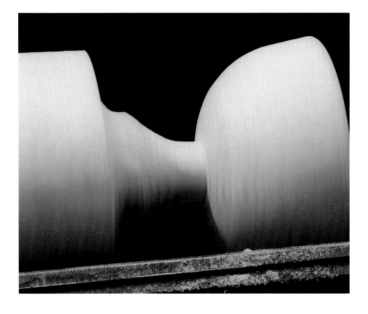

The rounded edge of the goblet bowl.

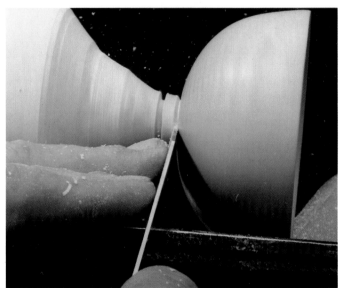

With a very thin parting tool, begin to apply a bead just below the bowl.

Sand the exterior of the goblet, using a dust extractor to keep the air clean.

Sweep up to the bead with the bowl gouge. We want the foot diameter to be about 3/4 of the size of the bowl.

As the stem gets thinner, support it with your hand as you work with the gouge.

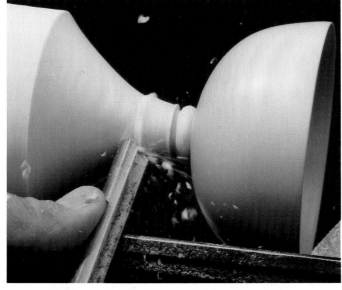 

When the stem is properly reduced, use the parting tool to begin to separate the base from the waste wood.

Round down the edge of the base to match the bead on the stem.

Sand the stem and foot smooth. Apply Danish Oil (or any sealer your prefer) to the stem and base.

Now part off the piece. Again we are in a deep groove so we must keep the groove wider than the parting tool to avoid binding. You need to shorten your grip on the tool since you are using it one handed and need to maintain firm control. Use the other hand to support the piece as you part.

It is important to seal the wood so that the following layers of wax do not continue to soak into the material. Sealing the wood also allows you to build up a high shine if required with subsequent layers.

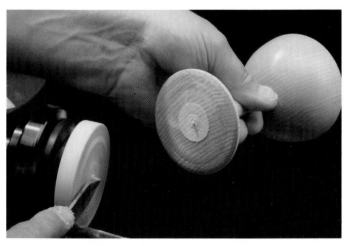

A goblet is born. Sand the base smooth on a disc or belt sander and apply a finish of your choice.

Straw-Stemmed Goblet

A Straw-Stemmed Goblet:

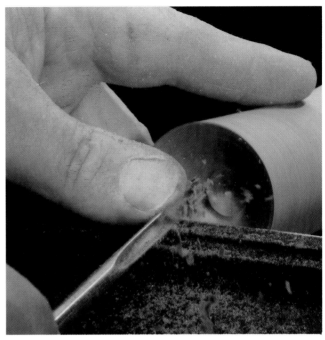

Using a 12" long 2 x 2 of American Black Walnut, we are going to make a straw stemmed goblet. Follow the same instructions for rounding down the block and fitting it to the chuck. Using a much smaller bowl gouge, round down the inside of the goblet bowl.

Rounding down the inside of the goblet bowl.

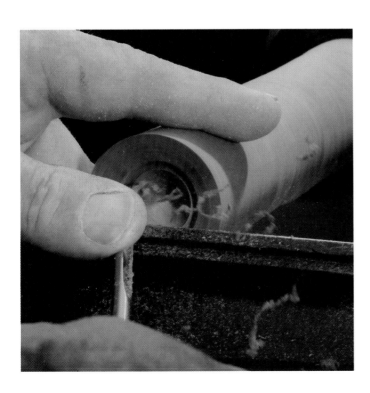

The rounded bowl.

Using the spinning lathe, extend the mark around the bowl.

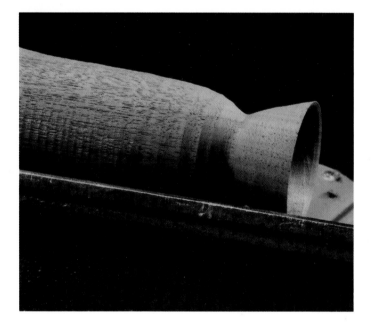

Using a small roughing gouge, reduce the outside of the goblet to an open bowl shape.

Finish rounding down the bowl as before.

Using a depth gauge, transfer the depth of the goblet bowl to the outside of the bowl. Mark the depth in pencil.

Smooth down the bowl as before with the cloth backed abrasives.

Finish sanding the bowl now, both inside and outside. Once you start to make the thin straw stem, you will not be able to touch the bowl again.

Place a piece of paper towel within the bowl and use the tail stock to hold it in place. This will provide greater support while reducing the stem to 1/8" in diameter down its entire length. Note: do not stop the lathe now until the goblet is finished. The thrust when restarting the lathe may break this delicate leg.

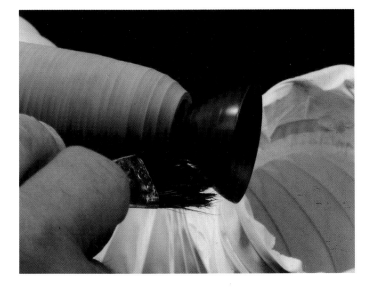

Apply Danish Oil to the bowl and rub it down with a paper towel until you have a glossy surface.

Reduce the stem at the base of the bowl with the parting tool. Finishing rounding the bowl base as well.

Apply wax over the oil to make it shine.

Sanding the base of the bowl smooth.

Use the parting gouge to straighten and smooth off the shaft.

This is the diameter of the stem. If all goes well, this stem will be 8" long.

Continue reducing the stem an inch at a time.

Gradually reduce the wood stock to the stem thickness with the bowl gouge.

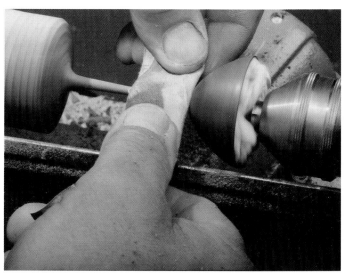

Sanding finishes dimensioning the piece, finish as you move down the length of the stem.

Continue moving down the shaft. Finish the leg with Danish Oil as you go.

Reminder: don't turn off the lathe until you reach the end of this piece. Turning the lathe back on would risk breaking the stem. Keep the lathe running and continue to reduce the wood.

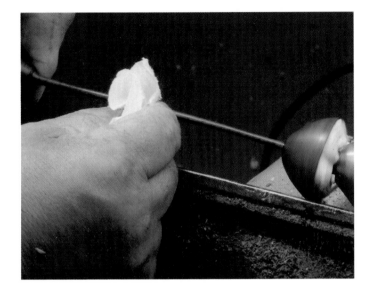

Carefully applying the oil.

Parting the foot.

Reduce the foot to a trumpet shape with the small bowl gouge. The trumpet shape works well with this spindly sort of goblet. The extra weight of the wood in this type of foot adds stability to this tall goblet.

The trumpet foot is reduced.

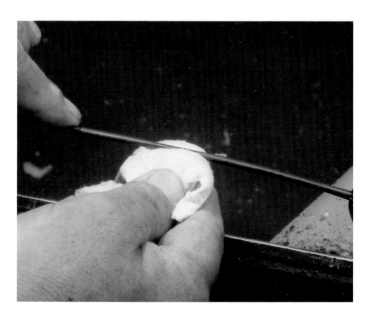

Sand the foot and the stem down one last time.

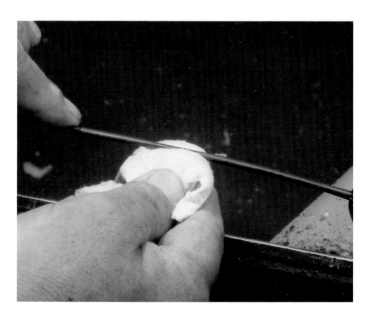

Gently apply your finishing coat.

Parting the goblet from the tail stock. Lightly sand the base to get it level and you are done. Sand the base of the foot on a disc or belt sander. Apply the finish of your choice.

A Chalice in Three Pieces

Using American Black Walnut, we going to be making a three piece chalice. The round top and bottom pieces measure 5" in diameter. They are 2" thick disks. The stem measures 6" long x 1 1/2" square. A 2" thick disk is fine for a high trumpet foot, 1 1/2" will suffice for the lower foot we will make here. **Note:** 2" thick wood for a trumpet foot, less for flatter designs.

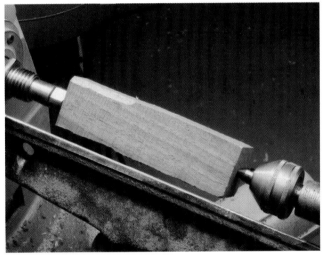

Place the stem block on the lathe between centres.

Using the 3/4" roughing gouge, round down the block.

Like this.

Reduce the tenons with the parting tool.

Mark off your tenons, approximaely 3/8" in length.

Measuring with the calipers as the wood is reduced.

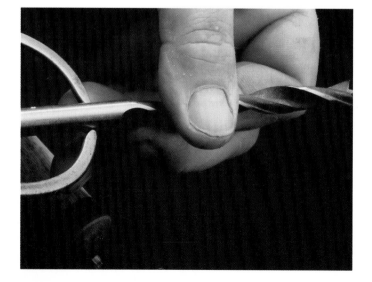

The size of the drill bit measures 3/8" in diameter. Measure with the calipers and reduce the tenons to this size.

Widening the opening with the parting gouge.

Reducing the remaining wood of the tenon.

Both tenons have been reduced.

The reduced tenon. Round the corners for a nice fit.

Form a bead on the base of the goblet leg, which is rolled over using the parting tool.

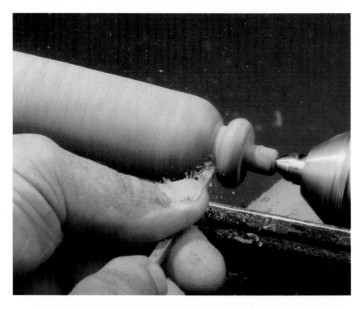

Follow this with a small cove between these items made with a small round nosed scraper.

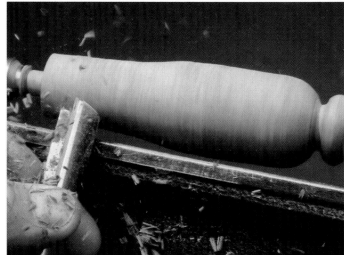

Round over the end on the bottom of the leg using the same method.

Taper the leg to suit the overall proportion. Determine the dimension of the top of the leg to form a bead under the top of the chalice bowl.

Forming the bead.

Use a 1/2" roughing gouge to make a neat little hollow in the wood. Remember to work down hill to keep the grain smooth. Working up hill is like stroking a cat the wrong way, the cat's fur or the wood's grain will be raised and rough.

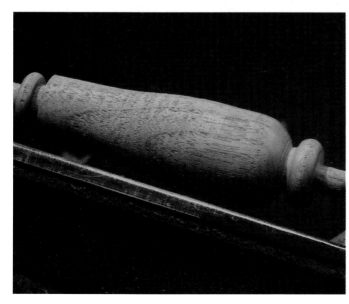

The baluster stem with beads and tenons.

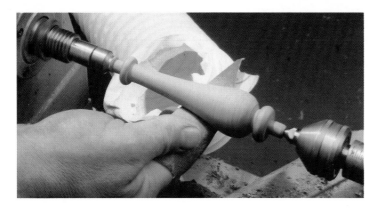

Using the abrasive, smooth down the stem. Remember to follow your contours so as not to lose them. Respect them.

Oil and wax the stem.

Remember not to get any oil or wax on the tenons as we need them to be clean to glue.

Use shavings to burnish the piece.

I have turned the stem around to reduce this small lip on the end of the tenon. I could not reach it from the other end.

Reduce this lip with the parting tool.

Like so. Repeat to create the holes for the tenons in both the base and the bowl.

Place guide holes in the centres of the base and bowl with an awl before drilling.

Lock in the screw chuck.

Using a 3/8" drill bit, drill your hole roughly 1" deep, or to suit the tenon you have prepared.

Screw the bowl blank in place first.

True up the edge with a 3/8" bowl gouge, rubbing the bevel and cutting along. Stop just before reaching the edge of the wood. The reason is that if we continue with this cut we will split the end grain of the wood on the face.

We will pick up this ridge by coming back the other way.

Repeat this process moving in the other direction.

Like so.

Angle the tool rest and cut away a 45 degree champher on the corner of the disc.

Measure 2 1/4" on the dividers to obtain the size for the spigot which will hold the chalice bowl when we turn it around.

Gradually cut away at an angle with the 3/8" bowl gouge and create the undershape of the chalice.

Clean up the flat face on the bottom of the chalice bowl with the 1/2" roughing gouge.

Now we are going to mark out the spigot with the dividers. When marking out the spigot, place the left leg of the dividers directly on the tool rest. Score a fine line with the left leg only, taking care not to let the right leg touch the wood. The right side is against the upward rotation of the wood and if the right leg catches, it will spin over. Always set out on the total diameter, never on the radius because if you are 1/16" out on the radius of the marking, you will be 1/8" out on the diameter. This will be most important to you if you have a standard wood turning chuck (which is not of the scroll type), where accurate dimensions are essential.

Create the spigot with the parting tool. First cut the spigot straight in 1/8" deep.

Then roll the edge of the bowl.

52

The spigot measures 1/8" deep and is used for holding the bowl when we reverse it and hollow out the inside. This spigot will be removed in a later process.

We are going to drill a hole to fit this tenon.

Place tape on the bit at the maximum depth you wish to cut, approximately 3/8" deep. We can't make this hole too deep or we will have to leave too much wood in the base of the chalice bowl.

Drilling the hole.

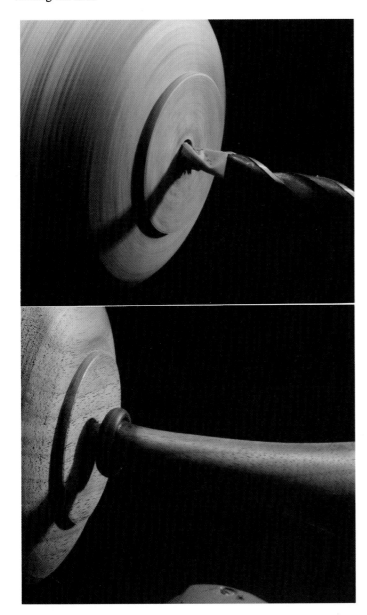

The tenon fits snugly in place.

Make a more refined shape along the outside of the chalice, similar to a champagne glass. Use the bowl gouge.

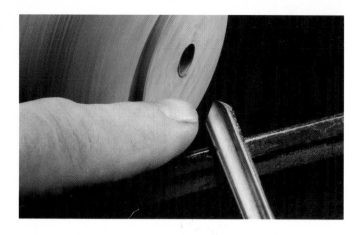

Using the inside edge of a 3/8" spindle gouge, I'm going to clean up the surface of the wood to remove any fine lines left by the bowl gouge. Doing this, we are actually using a burr of metal on the inside of the gouge that is left during the sharpening process.

Mount the spigot end to the screw chuck and prepare to hollow out the bowl.

Smoothing down the sides, removing lines.

Remove the bowl from the screw chuck.

Clean off the end.

Take off the edge.

Begin to round down the centre.

Round off the outer edge, beginning at the outside and sweeping in.

A double ended caliper is an excellent tool for determining the thickness of bowls, goblets, and hollow forms.

Sand the inside and the outside of the chalice bowl.

Using this measurement, reduce the bowl down to the centre, being careful not to cut too deeply, causing the screw hole to pop through. Far better to have a chalice a little too thick rather than to have one with a hole in it.

Coat with Danish Oil or the sealer of your choice.

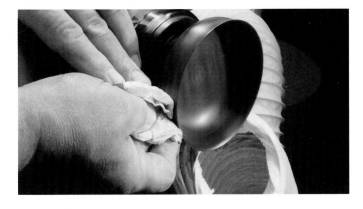

Buff the oil dry with a paper towel.

Add a little wax for gloss.

Now attach the base to the screw chuck and turn it out as we did with the bowl.

Clean up the bottom face.

We are going to make a shallow recess this time to use the chuck in its expansion mode. Mark out the size of the recess with the dividers.

Start cutting in the recess to a depth of no more than 1/8" (there is a tendency with many turners to make these recesses too big and ugly which spoils the look of their work). Start on the line, going in 1/8" deep using the full width of the parting tool. In the next cut, half of the parting tool overlaps the previous cut until the tool bottoms out at the depth of the last cut.

Repeat this process two or three times.

Remove the final piece of wood in the middle with a roughing gouge to complete the recess.

If you look at the side of the chuck jaws, you will see that they are flared. It is important to match the angle of the flare on the base.

When making a trumpet shaped foot, you must use nice smooth body motions, keeping the gouge bevel against the wood at all times.

Parting the foot.

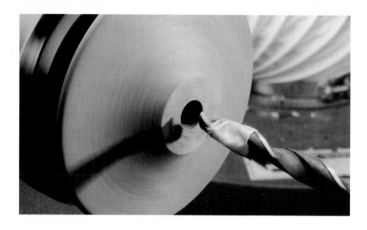

Drill the hole for the tenon in the foot.

Remove the base. Using a wad of paper toweling for padding, secure the goblet bowl in the lathe.

Put the goblet together. We need to snug down the bead a little closer.

Use a small bowl gouge (1/4" or 3/8") to remove the spigot from the bowl.

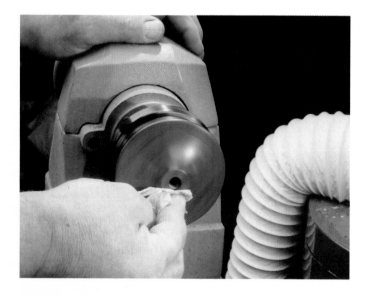

Sand the foot. Apply a coat of Danish Oil or sealer, buff dry, and wax to finish the base.

Sand the base of the bowl. Apply oil and wax to the bowl.

The completed projects

Gallery

The finished chalice.

A fluted goblet in Imbuya.

The taller goblet is turned from Laburnum by the author. The shorter
goblet is turned from ash by Brian Clifford.

Twisted stem goblets by Geoff Hughes.

A graceful goblet in sycamore by an unknown English turner.

Tiny goblets in a variety of woods by the author.

Natural top goblet in English Yew Wood by the author.

Suppliers

Wood turners may contact the following suppliers to have their
needs met:

Middlesex Woodcraft Centre
70 Woodend Green Road
Hayes
Middlesex
England
UB3 2SL
Phone: 0181 561 5885
Fax: 0181 561 5770
(Courses in wood turning, carving, and pyrography for
beginners are offered here as well.)